1 MONTH OF
FREE
READING

at
www.ForgottenBooks.com

By purchasing this book you are eligible for one month membership to ForgottenBooks.com, giving you unlimited access to our entire collection of over 1,000,000 titles via our web site and mobile apps.

To claim your free month visit:

www.forgottenbooks.com/free906100

ISBN 978-0-266-89601-2
PIBN 10906100

Historic, archived document

Do not assume content reflects current
scientific knowledge, policies, or practices.

WINTER - 1914 - SPRING

Office, Packing House, Commissary and Station at Chase

BULLETIN NO. 1

CHASE, ALABAMA, JANUARY 15, 1914.

TO THE TRADE:

Orders for this surplus stock will be booked in rotation as received. Can ship immediately, or will hold for spring shipment.

Our imported Seedlings are now in transit from Europe; apple and Japan Pear Seedlings have arrived and can ship on an hour's notice.

Note our complete list of Shrubs, Ornamental Trees, Climbers, etc., for transplanting, under the heading "Lining Out" Stock. Your orders for this class of stock should be sent in NOW. Note also the light grade peach, plum, apricot, etc., for transplanting to nursery row.

Note our list of Nurserymen's Supplies—French Pruning Shears, Waxed Grafting Thread, Fumigating Chemicals, and many items not easily located elsewhere. Supply orders shipped next train after receipt of order.

Please name second choice where possible.

Terms and conditions of sale as per our regular trade list, copy on request.

Cash with order where purchaser's credit is unknown to us.

Boxing extra except as noted.

Freight prepaid to our distributing points—Rochester, St. Louis and Philadelphia—when shipments can be included in our regular car lots to these points.

Yours very truly,

CHASE NURSERY COMPANY

CHASE, ALABAMA

PEACH, June Buds

	2 to 3 feet	18 to 24 ins.	12 to 18 ins.	6 to 12 ins.
Price per M—	$25.00	$20.00	$15.00	$12.50
Alexander		125	25	50
Arp Beauty			1325	500
Belle of Georgia			3275	850
Bilyeus Oct.	3365	1575	75	
Bishops Early	2125	1075	450	150
Carman	700	5600	6000	100
Champion	2125	3800	1825	
Crawfords Early		325	175	
Crawfords Late			350	200
ELBERTA		3000	26000	1300
Fox Seedling	825	3650	2325	650
Greensboro		120	850	
Heath Cling		525	525	50
Hiley		500		600
Krummels Oct.	75	625		
Lemon Cling		290	290	
Mayflower	1180	2900	3700	
Salway	1700	4700	2325	
Slappey	50	550	425	
Sunrise Cling	175	1800	975	350
Victor			1100	850
Walkers Var. Free	1000	1200	700	350

PLUM, on Myrobolan, 2 Year

	4 to 6 feet 9-16 to ⅝ 12½c	4 to 5 feet ½ to 9-16 10c	3 to 4 feet under ½ 8c
French Prune		26	38
German Prune	160	80	
Shippers Pride	40		
Yellow Egg	30	18	

PLUM, on Myrobolan, 1 Year

	3 to 4 feet 6½c	2 to 3 feet 5c	1 to 2 feet 3½c
Abundance		174	75
Burbank		670	260
Red June		277	87
Wickson	225	195	157
Wild Goose	376	950	496

PLUM, on Peach, 1 Year

	3 to 4 feet 6½c	2 to 3 feet 5c	1 to 2 feet 3½c
Abundance		225	
Burbank		700	
Red June	700	1300	475
Shropshire Damson		225	
Wickson	350	550	150

PLUM, on Peach, June Budded

	3 to 4 feet 6½c	2 to 3 feet 5c	18 to 24 ins. 3½c	12 to 18 ins. 2½c	6 to 12 ins. 2c
Burbank	233	1175	615	105	
Red June	329	1150	600	200	300

QUINCE, 2 Year

	9-16 to ⅝ 4 to 5 ft. 17½c	½ to 9-16 3 to 5 ft. 15c
Borgeat	65	70
Champion	40	60
Meech	20	
Orange		100

4

MULBERRY, I Year, Mostly Whips

	6 to 8 feet	5 to 6 feet	4 to 5 feet	3 to 4 feet	2 to 3 feet
Price per 100—	$20.00	$17.50	$12.50	$7.50	$5.00
Black English	150	50	140	....	145
Hicks	....	65	195	280	445

FIGS

	4 to 5 feet	3 to 4 feet	2 to 3 feet	1 to 2 feet
Price per 100—	$15.00	$12.50	$8.00	$5.00
Black Ischia	10	23	10	....
Blue Genoa	30	18	19	....
Brown Turkey	15	70	125	121
Celestial	225	1000	2200	2600
Magnolia	....	....	400	....
White Adriatic	60	180	95	77

These Figs were cellared after first frost, are Sound to Tips.

GRAPE VINES, 2 Year, New York Grown

	Each			Each
700 Concord No. 1	2¾ cts.	700 Moores Diamond No. 2		3½ cts.
3000 Concord No. 2	2 cents	100 Moores Early No. 1		4½ cts.
75 Catawba No. 1	4 cents	300 Moores Early No. 2		3½ cts.
150 Catawba No. 2	3 cents	100 Niagara No. 1		4½ cts.
300 Delaware No. 2	3½ cts.	50 Niagara No. 2		3½ cts.
350 Ives Seedling No. 1	4 cents	80 Worden No. 1		4½ cts.
3000 Ives Seedling No. 2	2¾ cts.	300 Worden No. 2		3½ cts.
1500 Lutie No. 2	6 cents	1000 Scupernong, White, No. 1		10 cents
400 Moores Diamond, No. 1	4½ cts.	250 Scuppernong, James Black, No. 1		12½ cts.

SATSUMA ORANGE, I Year, on Trifoliata

NOTE—Direct shipment only from our contract grower in Florida.

300 Satsuma Orange, 3 to 4 feet		35c
550 Satsuma Orange, 2 to 3 feet		20c
850 Satsuma Orange, 1 to 2 feet		15c

POMEGRANATE, Spanish Ruby, I Year

25	2 to 3 feet	17½c
130	18 to 24 inches	15c
120	12 to 18 inches	12c

NUT TREES

	Per 100
50 Almond IXL, 5 to 6 feet	$20 00
14 Almond IXL, 3 to 4 feet	12 50
50 Almond IXL, 2 to 3 feet	7 50
20 Almond, Ne Plus Ultra, 3 to 4 feet	12 50
100 Almond, Ne Plus Ultra, 2 to 3 feet	7 50
25 Almond, Ne Plus Ultra, 18 to 24 inches	6 00
600 Almond, Soft Shell, Seedlings, 1 to 2 feet	4 00
100 Chestnut, Japan Mammoth, 2 to 3 feet, branched	25 00
100 Chestnut, Japan Mammoth, 18 to 24 inches, branched	15 00
50 Chestnut, Spanish, 5 to 6 feet, well branched	20 00
50 Chestnut, Spanish, 4 to 5 feet, well branched	15 00
500 Pecan Seedlings, 18 to 24 inches, whips	8 00
900 Pecan Seedlings, 12 to 18 inches, whips	5 00
1200 Pecan Seedlings, 6 to 12 inches, whips	3 50
Pecans, Grafted—see below	
50 Walnut, Black, 4 to 5 feet, whips	20 00
100 Walnut, Black, 3 to 4 feet, whips	15 00
200 Walnut, Black, 2 to 3 feet, whips	7 00
540 Walnut, English, 18 to 24 inches, whips	10 00
2200 Walnut, English, 12 to 18 inches, whips	6 00
780 Walnut, English, 6 to 12 inches, whips	3 00
740 Walnut, Japan, 3 to 4 feet, whips	15 00
430 Walnut, Japan, 2 to 3 feet, whips	10 00
1050 Walnut, Japan, 18 to 24 inches, whips	7 00
2325 Walnut, Japan, 12 to 18 inches, whips	5 00
1875 Walnut, Japan, 6 to 12 inches, whips	3 00

5

PECANS, Grafted and Budded

NOTE—We can often make shipment direct from our contract growers in Florida and South Alabama and save our southern customers something in express and freight charges.

450 Assorted, 3 to 4 feet	60c
1100 Assorted, 2 to 3 feet	50c
450 Assorted, 1 to 2 feet	40c

Stuart Delmas Van Deman

SMALL FRUITS

	Per 1000
10000 Asparagus, 2 year Crowns	$ 6 00
300 Rhubarb, 1 year	27 50
400 Currants, Wilder Red, No. 1	30 00
500 Gooseberry, Houghton, 1 year, No. 1	40 00
2000 Cuthbert Raspberry, No. 1	8 50
750 Plum Farmer, Blackcap, T-P	20 00
1200 Plum Farmer, Blackcap, Tips	12 50
1100 Kansas Blackcap Tips	12 50
1000 Cumberland Blackcap Tips	12 50
1000 Snyder Blackberry, Root Cutting Plants	12 50
2000 Ohmer Blackberry, Root Cutting Plants	12 50
1000 Austin Dewberry	12 50
200 Japanese Wineberry, Tips	20 00

STRAWBERRY PLANTS

Our Strawberry Plants are grown on contract by one of the best growers in the Chattanooga district and will be shipped direct. Can supply the following five varieties which we name in their order of ripening:

1 Lady Thompson   2 Klondyke   3 Aroma   4 Tenn. Favorite   5 Gandy
Price per 1000, f. o. b. Chattanooga, $2.25

PEACH SEED

Crop 1912, Local Seedling Seed, f. o. b. here, per bushel	$1 75

Sixty-two bushels large peach seed, supposed to be all Elberta seed, immediate shipment, F. O. B. HERE, per bushel, 75 cents.

SCIONS

A limited supply of the following Pear Scions, no charge for packing:

Pear Scions, per M $3 50

Bartlett	Early Harvest	Kieffer	Le Conte
Clapps Favorite	Garber	Koonce	Magnolia
Duchess	Japan Golden Russett	Lawrence	Wilders Early

CLIMBERS, 2 Year, Except as Noted

	Per 100
50 Ampelopsis, Muralis	$10 00
150 Ampelopsis, Quinquefolia	7 00
200 Ampelopsis, Veitchii	12 00
50 Clematis, Henryii	17 50
100 Clematis, Jackmanii	16 00
25 Clematis, Mad. Andre	17 50
150 Clematis, Paniculata	10 00
200 Euonymus, Radicans	10 00
50 Lonicera, Flava, (Yellow Trumpet Honeysuckle)	10 00
500 Lonicera, Punicea. (Scarlet Trumpet Honeysuckle) 1year	5 00
250 Wistaria, Sinensis, (Seedlings)	12 50
200 Wistaria, Sinensis Alba, 3 year layered	20 00
150 Wistaria, Magnifica, (Seedlings)	10 00

SHRUBS

- All Shrubs offered are well grown in wide rows and are shapely, well branched plants.

	Per 100
ALTHEA, See Page 8	
50 Amorpha Fruticosa, 5 to 6 ft. --------	$12 50
50 Amorpha Fruticosa. 18 to 24 ins. ------	6 00
155 Amygdalus Nana Alba, 2 to 3 ft. ------	15 00
(White Almond)	
25 Amygdalus Nana Rosea, 2 to 3 ft. ------	15 00
(Pink Almond)	
50 Amygdalus Nana Rosea, 18 to 24 ins.	12 50
75 Amygdalus Nana Rosea, 12 to 18 ins.	10 00
25 Aralia Pentaphylla, 18 to 24 ins. ------	7 50
50 Aralia Pentaphylla, 12 to 18 ins. --------	5 00
100 Aronia Floribunda, 12 to 18 ins. --------	5 C0
100 Berberis Purpurea, 2 to 3 ft. -----------	8 00
300 Berberis Purpurea, 18 to 24 ins. -------	6 00
1200 Berberis Purpurea, 12 to 18 ins. --------	3 00
300 Berberis Thunbergii, 24 to 30 ins. ------	12 50
200 Berberis Vulgaris, 18 to 24 ins. --------	8 00
200 Berberis Vulgaris, 12 to 18 ins. ---------	3 00
50 Buddleia Lindleyana, 2 to 3 ft. ---------	10 00
75 Buddleia Lindleyana, 18 to 24 ins. ------	7 50
50 Caragana Arborescens, 2 to 3 ft. ------	6 00
100 Caragana Arborescens, 18 to 24 ins. ----	4 00
200 Calycanthus Floridus, 2 to 3 ft. ------	9 00
150 Calycanthus Floridus, 18 to 24 ins. ------	7 00
300 Caryopteris Mastacanthus, 12 to 18 ins.	6 00
150 Cephalanthus Occidentalis, 18 to 24 ins.	6 00
75 Colutea Arborescens, 2 to 3 ft. --------	7 50
100 Colutea Arborescens, 18 to 24 ins. ------	5 00
50 Cornus Paniculata, 18 to 24 ins. -------	10 00
75 Cornus Sanguinea, 18 to 24 ins. --------	7 50
200 Craetagus Oxyacantha, 2 to 3 ft. ------	8 00
300 Cydonia Japonica, 2 to 3 ft. -----------	10 00
300 Cydonia Japonica. 18 to 24 ins. ----------	7 50
50 Deutzia Candidissima, 3 to 4 ft. --------	10 00
100 Deutzia Candidissima, 2 to 3 ft. --------	7 50
100 Deutzia Scabra, 18 to 24 ins. ----------	7 50
100 Deutzia Crenata, Fl. Pl. Rosea, 2 to 3 ft.	7 50
50 Deutzia Fortunei, 3 to 4 ft. -----------	10 00
150 Deutzia Fortunei, 2 to 3 ft. -----------	7 50
200 Deutzia Fortunei, 18 to 24 ins. ---------	5 00
150 Deutzia, Pride of Rochester, 3 to 4 ft.	10 00
600 Deutzia, Pride of Rochester, 2 to 3 ft.	7 50
900 Deutzia, Pride of Rochester, 18 to 24 ins	5 00
100 Eleagnus Angustifolia, 3 to 4 ft. --------	10 00
250 Eleagnus Angustifolia, 2 to 3 ft. --------	7 50
200 Eleagnus Longipes, 2 to 3 ft. ----------	7 50
200 Eleagnus Longipes, 18 to 24 ins. -------	5 00
100 Exochorda Grandiflora, 4 to 5 ft. -----	15 00
150 Exochorda Grandiflora, 3 to 4 ft. -----	12 50
50 Exochorda Grandiflora, 2 to 3 ft. -----	10 00
100 Forsythia Intermedia, 2 to 3 ft. --------	8 00
200 Forsythia Suspensa, 3 to 4 ft. ----------	12 50
50 Forsythia Viridissima, 2 to 3 ft. ------	8 00
75 Hamamelis Virginiana, 2 to 3 ft. ------	12 50
450 Hydrangea P. G., 18 to 24 ins. ---------	10 00
1850 Hydrangea P. G., 12 to 18 ins. ---------	5 00
125 Hypericum Moserianum, 18 to 24 ins.	15 00
200 Indigofera Dosua. 2 to 3 ft. ------------	10 00
50 Jasminum Nudiflorum, 2 to 3 ft. -------	10 00
100 Jasminum Nudiflorum, 18 to 24 ins. ----	7 50
50 Jasminum Officinale, 3 to 4 ft. ----------	10 C0
150 Jasminum Officinale, 2 to 3 ft. --------	8 00
640 Lagerstroemia Indica, 2 to 3 ft. -------	15 00
(Crepe Myrtle)	
570 Lagerstroemia Indica, 18 to 24 ins. ---	10 00
750 Lagerstroemia Indica. 12 to 18 ins. ----	7 50
300 Lonicera Fragrantissima, 18 to 24 ins.	10 00
50 Lonicera Ledebouri; 18 to 24 ins. ------	10 C0

	Per 100
100 Lonicera Morrowii, 3 to 4 ft. ---------	12 50
150 Lonicera Morrowii, 2 to 3 ft. ---------	10 00
140 Lonicera Tartarica Alba, 12 to 18 ins.	6 00
100 Philadelphus Grandiflora, 3 to 4 ft. ----	12 50
250 Philadelphus Grandiflora, 2 to 3 ft. ----	10 00
150 Philadelphus Mont Blanc, 18 to 24 ins.	8 00
150 Prunus Triloba, 18 to 24 ins. ----------	10 00
100 Prunus Triloba, 12 to 18 ins. -----------	7 00
100 Rhodotypus Kerroides, 18 to 24 ins ----	8 00
50 Rhus Aromatica, 3 to 4 ft. ------------	20 00
50 Rhus Aromatica, 2 to 3 ft. ------------	15 00
150 Rhus Cotinus, 3 to 4 ft. --------------	10 00
350 Rhus Cotinus, 2 to 3 ft. ---------------	8 00
100 Rhus Cotinus, 18 to 24 ins. ------------	6 00
150 Rhus Typhina Laciniata, 18 to 24 ins.	10 00
100 Robinia Hispida, 3 to 4 ft. ------------	15 00
100 Robinia Hispida, 2 to 3 ft. ------------	10 00
50 Sambucus Nigra, 2 to 3 ft. ------------	7 50
100 Sambucus Nigra, 18 to 24 ins. ---------	6 00
50 Sambucus Nigra Laciniata, 2 to 3 ft.	10 00
50 Sambucus Racemosus, 18 to 24 ins. ----	6 00
100 Spirea Arguta, 2 to 3 ft. --------------	10 00
150 Spirea Arguta, 18 to 24 ins. -----------	8 00
200 Spirea Ariaefolia, 18 to 24 ins. --------	8 00
100 Spirea Bumalda, 18 to 24 ins. ---------	8 00
200 Spirea Bumalda, 15 to 18 ins. ---------	5 00
300 Spirea Callosa Alba, 15 to 18 ins. --------	8 00
100 Spirea Callosa Rosea, 3 to 4 ft. --------	10 00
250 Spirea Callosa Rosea, 2 to 3 ft. --------	7 C0
150 Spirea Douglasi Rosea, 18 to 24 ins. ---	7 00
150 Spirea Opulifolia Aurea, 18 to 24 ins.	6 00
50 Spirea Prunifolia Fl. Pl. 2 to 3 ft. -----	10 00
100 Spirea Prunifolia Fl. Pl. 18 to 24 ins. ----	8 00
50 Spirea Reevesiana Fl. Pl. 2 to 3 ft. -----	8 00
50 Spirea Thunbergii, 2 to 3 ft. ----------	12 50
400 Spirea Thunbergii, 12 to 18 ins. --------	8 00
100 Stephanandra Flexuosa, 2 to 3 ft. ------	10 00
50 Symphoricarpos Racemosus, 2 to 3 ft.	10 00
100 Symphoricarpos Racemosus, 18 to 24 in	8 00
300 Symphoricarpos Vulgaris, 2 to 3 ft. ---	6 00
500 Symphoricarpos Vulgaris, 18 to 24 ins.	4 00
25 Syringa Japonica, 3 to 4 ft. ----------	20 00
50 Syringa Japonica, 2 to 3 ft. ----------	15 00
25 Syringa Josikea, 2 to 3 ft. ------------	15 00
20 Syringa Pekinensis, 3 to 4 ft. ---------	20 00
125 Syringa Persica Alba, 2 to 3 ft. -------	15 00
100 Syringa Persica Alba, 18 to 24 ins. ------	10 00
30 Syringa Rothamagensis. 3 to 4 ft. ------	20 00
150 Syringa Rothamagensis, 2 to 3 ft. ------	15 C0
50 Syringa Villosa, 3 to 4 ft. ------------	15 00
150 Syringa Villosa, 2 to 3 ft. ------------	12 50
300 Syringa Vulgaris, 18 to 24 ins. ---------	6 00
200 Syringa Vulgaris Alba, 12 to 18 ins. ----	5 00
25 Tamarix Hispida Estivalis, 4 to 5 ft. ----	20 00
50 Tamarix Hispida Estivalis. 2 to 3 ft. ----	12 50
100 Tamarix Hispida Estivalis, 18 to 24 ins.	10 00
25 Tamarix Japonica Plumosa, 3 to 4 ft,	12 50
25 Tamarix Japonica Plumosa, 2 to 3 ft.	10 00
25 Tamarix Japonica Plumosa, 18 to 24 in.	8 C0
20 Virburnum Opulus, 3 to 4 ft. ---------	15 00
75 Weigelia Candida, 3 to 4 ft. -----------	12 50
100 Weigelia Candida, 2 to 3 ft. -----------	10 00
100 Weigelia Candida, 18 to 24 ins. --------	8 00
150 Weigelia Eve Rathke, 18 to 24 ins. -------	10 00
100 Weigelia Rosea, 2 to 3 ft. -------------	10 00
150 Weigelia Rosea, 18 to 24 ins. -----------	8 00

ALTHEA, Bush Form

Price per 100—	3 to 4 feet Well Br $10.00	2 to 3 feet Well Br $7.50	18 to 24 ins. Well Br $4.00	12 to 18 ins. Well Br $2.50
Admiral Dewey	....	250	1600	800
Amplissima	....	....	400	600
Anemonaeflorus	....	600	1200	1600
Ardens	250	300	800	600
Boule de Feu	....	300	450	800
Carneus Plenus	....	350	900	850
Duchess de Brabant	....	220	1150	1200
Jeanne de Arc	300	350	400	600
Monstrosus	....	600	1400	900
Rubis	200	400	1100	850
Souv. Chas. Breton	150	200	400	600
Speciosa	....	250	500	700

ALTHEA, Tree Form

Price per 100—	¾ to 1 inch 6 to 8 feet $20.00	⅝ to ¾ inch 5 to 6 feet $15.00	9-16 to ⅝ in. 4 to 5 feet $12.50	½ to 9-16 in. 3½ to 5 feet $10.00
Amplissima	....	....	25	110
Anemonaeflorus	....	....	100	197
Boule de Feu	....	35	215	185
Carneus Plenus	....	105	123	40
Jeanne de Arc	....	50	40	20
Monstrosus	160	100	18	....
Souv. Chas. Breton	85	75	160	110
Speciosa	90	92	50	30

ALTHEA SPECIAL, Single Pure White

Price per 100—	2 to 3 feet Well Br $10.00	18 to 24 ins. Well Br $7.50	12 to 18 ins. Well Br $4.00
SNOWDRIFT	200	800	700
TOTUS ALBUS	450	2200	1500

(For description of Althea see our regular Trade List)

SPIREA VAN HOUTTE

		Per 1000
5000	1 year, 18 to 24 inches, Selected, well branched	$25 00
11000	1 year, 12 to 18 inches, Selected, well branched	20 00
22000	1 year, 1 to 2 feet, well rooted, for transplanting	17 50

Our 1 to 2 feet Spirea Van Houtte is stronger, better rooted and heavier than imported stock of same height.

PRIVET

		Per 1000
18000	Amoor River North, transplanting	$20 00
13000	Amoor River North, 12 to 18 inches, 2 canes	25 00
6000	Amoor River North, 12 to 18 inches, 3 canes and up	30 00
3000	Amoor River North, 18 to 24 inches, 2 canes	30 00
1600	Amoor River South, transplanting	17 50
3800	Amoor River South, 12 to 18 inches	20 00
6300	Amoor River South, 18 to 24 inches	22 50
6100	Amoor River South, 2 to 3 feet	25 00
800	Amoor River South, 3 to 4 feet	35 00
26000	California Privet, transplanting	7 50
6000	California Privet, 6 to 12 inches, well branched	8 50
3000	Ibota Privet, transplanting	17 50
2000	Ibota Privet, 12 to 18 inches, well branched	25 00
500	Regelianum Privet, 12 to 18 inches	70 00
300	CALIFORNIA PRIVET, TREE FORM, 4 to 5 feet, Price, each	20 cents

Per 100

Apple, Flowering, 3 to 4 feet _____$17 50
100 Coronaria   75 Niedzwetzkyana
25 Floribunda   40 Spectabilis.
20 Scheideckeri   60 Floribunda Atr.

Apple Flowering, 2 to 3 feet _____ 12 50
250 Coronaria   100 Neidzwetzkyana
40 Floribunda   25 Scheideckeri
75 Floribunda Atrosanguinea

50 Aralia Spinosa, 6 to 8 feet _____ 25 00
75 5 to 6 feet _____ 20 00
60 4 to 5 feet _____ 15 00
50 Ash, American White, 8 to 10 feet _____ 25 00
100 6 to 8 feet _____ 17 50
60 Ash, European Mountain, 5 to 6 feet _____ 15 00
100 Birch, White, 10 to 12 ft. _____ 40 00
150 8 to 10 feet _____ 30 00
100 6 to 8 feet _____ 20 00
75 Birch, Cut Leaved, 8 to 10 feet _____ 70 00
50 6 to 8 feet _____ 50 00
220 Catalpa Bungeii, 1 year heads _____ 40 00
Catalpa Speciosa,
50 12 to 14 feet, 2 to 3½ inches _____ 50 00
100 10 to 12 feet, 1½ to 2 inches _____ 35 00
75 8 to 10 feet, 1 to 1½ inches _____ 25 00
60 6 to 8 feet _____ 15 00
100 5 to 6 feet _____ 10 00
Wild Cherry, (Prunus Serotina)
100 10 to 12 feet, 1½ to 2 inches _____ 45 00
60 8 to 10 feet _____ 35 00
50 Cercis Canadensis, 4 to 5 feet _____ 20 00
75 3 to 4 feet _____ 15 00
150 Cornus Florida, 2 to 3 feet _____ 15 00
Elm, American,
150 10 to 12 feet, 1½ to 1¾ inches _____ 50 00
250 8 to 10 feet, 1 to 1½ inches _____ 35 00
200 6 to 8 feet _____ 20 00
25 Empress Tree, 5 to 6 feet _____ 40 00
100 4 to 5 feet _____ 35 00
25 Ginkgo Biloba, 6 to 8 feet _____ 35 00
50 5 to 6 feet _____ 30 00
50 Larch, European, 8 to 10 feet _____ 40 00
25 6 to 8 feet _____ 30 00
200 Linden, American, 6 to 8 feet _____ 35 00
150 Locust, Black, 8 to 10 feet _____ 15 00
200 6 to 8 feet _____ 10 00
80 Magnolia, G. F. 4 to 5 feet _____ 75 00
210 3 to 4 feet _____ 40 00
160 2 to 3 feet _____ 30 00
120 18 to 24 inches _____ 25 00
25 Magnolia, Hypoleuca, 8 to 10 feet _____ 50 00
40 6 to 8 feet _____ 40 00
30 5 to 6 feet _____ 30 00
20 4 to 5 feet _____ 25 00
20 Magnolia, Kobus, 8 to 10 feet _____ 50 00
30 6 to 8 feet _____ 40 00
60 5 to 6 feet _____ 30 00
25 4 to 5 feet _____ 25 00
60 Maple, Japan, Palmatum, 4 to 5 feet _____ 40 00
140 3 to 4 feet _____ 35 00
80 2 to 3 feet _____ 25 00

Maple, Norway,   Per 100
25 1¾ to 2 inches, 10 to 12 feet _____ 100 00
50 1½ to 1¾ inches, 8 to 10 feet _____ 60 00
40 1¼ to 1½ inches, 8 to 10 feet _____ 40 00
80 1 to 1¼ inches, 7 to 9 feet _____ 30 00
100 6 to 8 feet _____ 25 00
Maple, Silver,
250 2 to 2½ inches, 12 to 14 feet _____ 100 00
300 1½ to 2 inches, 10 to 12 feet _____ 50 00
200 1¼ to 1½ inches, 9 to 11 feet _____ 30 00
300 1 to 1¼ inches, 8 to 10 feet _____ 20 00
850 6 to 8 feet _____ 12 50
400 5 to 6 feet _____ 10 00
Maple, Sugar,
50 1½ to 1¾ inches, 10 to 12 feet _____ 100 00
75 1¼ to 1½ inches, 8 to 10 feet _____ 70 00
100 1 to 1¼ inches, 8 to 10 feet _____ 40 00
200 6 to 8 feet _____ 30 00
200 Maple, Weirs Cut Leaved, 6 to 8 feet ____ 20 00
300 5 to 6 feet _____ 15 00
150 Mulberry, Teas Weeping, 2 year heads ____ 50 00
50 Oak, Pin, 6 to 8 feet _____ 50 00
100 5 to 6 feet _____ 35 00
200 Peach, Double Red, 5 to 7 feet _____ 17 50
300 4 to 5 feet _____ 12 50
350 3 to 4 feet _____ 10 00
150 Peach, Double White, 5 to 7 feet _____ 17 50
350 4 to 5 feet _____ 12 50
300 3 to 4 feet _____ 10 00
75 Poplar, Bolleana, 10 to 12 feet _____ 30 00
100 8 to 10 feet _____ 20 00
50 6 to 8 feet _____ 15 00
Poplar, Carolina,
400 12 to 14 feet, 2 to 2½ inches _____ 30 00
500 10 to 12 feet, 1½ to 2 inches _____ 25 00
600 8 to 10 feet _____ 12 50
800 6 to 8 feet _____ 8 00
Poplar, Lombardy,
300 12 to 14 feet, 1½ to 2 inches _____ 35 00
400 10 to 12 feet, 1 to 1½ inches _____ 20 00
300 8 to 10 feet _____ 15 00
(These Lombardy are not low branched)
Poplar, Norway,
150 1 to 1½ inches, 10 to 12 feet _____ 20 00
300 8 to 10 feet _____ 15 00
350 6 to 8 feet _____ 8 00
Poplar, Tulip,
150 2 to 2½ inches, 12 to 14 feet _____ 75 00
100 1½ to 2 inches, 10 to 12 feet _____ 50 00
150 Prunus Pissardi, 4 to 5 feet _____ 15 00
5 3 to 4 feet _____ 12 50
Sycamore, American,
300 2 to 2½ inches, 12 to 14 feet _____ 50 00
500 1½ to 2 inches, 10 to 12 feet _____ 40 00
400 8 to 10 feet _____ 25 00
300 6 to 8 feet _____ 15 00
250 Umbrella, China, 4 to 5 feet _____ 15 00
1100 3 to 4 feet _____ 10 00
600 2 to 3 feet _____ 7 50
50 Willow, Babylonica, 6 to 8 feet _____ 15 00
100 5 to 6 feet _____ 12 50
125 4 to 5 feet _____ 10 00

EVERGREENS

See our regular Wholesale Catalogue.

ROSES—Own Roots

	Per 100
25 Alice Aldrich, No. 1	$10 00
50 Alice Aldrich, No. 2	7 50
40 Alfred Colomb, No. 1	12 50
40 Alfred Colomb, No. 2	8 00
100 Am. Pillar, No. 1	10 00
150 Am. Pillar, No. 2	7 50
220 Antoine Rivoire, No. 1	15 00
350 Antoine Rivoire, No. 2	10 50

BABY RAMBLERS

	Per 100
80 Jessie, No. 1	12 50
160 Jessie, No. 2	8 00
136 Mrs. Taft, No. 1	12 50
210 Mrs. Taft, No. 2	8 00
160 Mad. N. Levavaseur, No. 1	12 50
370 Mad. N. Levavasenr, No. 2	8 00
75 Balduin, (Helen Gould) No. 1	15 00
25 Balduin, (Helen Gould) No. 2	10 00
690 Blumenschmidt, No. 1	10 00
135 Blumenschmidt, No. 2	7 50
200 Bar. Le Duc, No. 1	7 50
300 Bar. Le Duc, No. 2	5 00
50 Cherokee, No. 1	12 50
50 Cherokee, No. 2	8 00
200 Clio, No. 2	8 00
600 Crimson Rambler, No. 1	12 50
800 Dorothy Perkins, No. 1	7 50
1500 Dorothy Perkins, No. 2	5 00
500 Empress of China, No. 1	7 50
100 Etoile de France, No. 2	10 00
80 Eugene Boullet, No. 1	12 50
90 Eugene Boullet, No. 2	8 00
600 Excelsa, No. 1	12 50
700 Excelsa, No. 2	8 00
300 Flower of Fairfield, No. 2	10 00
200 Freiherr Von Marschall, No. 1	12 50
300 Freiherr Von Marschall, No. 2	8 00
150 Gardenia, No. 2	8 00
250 Gen. Jack, No. 2	8 00
50 Goldfinch, No. 1	12 50
50 Goldfinch, No. 2	8 00
100 Hiawatha, No. 1	12 50
125 Hiawatha, No. 2	8 00

	Per 100
150 John Hopper, No. 2	$ 8 00
120 K. A. Victoria, No. 1	15 00
550 K. A. Victoria, No. 2	10 00
120 Killarney, No. 1	15 00
200 Killarney, No. 2	10 00
900 Lady Gay, No. 1	7 50
50 Mad. Masson, No. 2	10 00
17 Mme. Jennie Guillemot, No. 1	15 00
30 Mme. Jennie Guillemot, No. 2	10 00
600 Madam Plantier, No. 1	7 50
150 Magna Charta, No. 2	8 00
1100 Maman Cochet, No. 1	12 50
800 Maman Cochet, No. 2	8 00
200 Mrs. B. R. Cant, No. 1	12 50
150 Mrs. B. R. Cant, No. 2	8 00
110 Meteor, No. 1	12 50
200 Meteor, No. 2	8 00
300 Pink Rambler, No. 1	7 50
400 Paul Neyron, No. 2	8 00
300 Prince Camille, No. 2	8 00
400 Queen of Prairie, No. 1	7 50
150 Rhea Reid, No. 1	15 00
275 Rhea Reid, No. 2	10 00
1000 Rosa Wichuriana, No. 2	5 00
100 South Orange Perfection, No. 2	5 00
100 Tausendschon, No. 1	7 50
150 Tausendschon, No. 2	5 00
300 Tennessee Belle, No. 1	6 00
400 Tennessee Belle, No. 2	4 00
50 Trier, No. 1	10 00
50 Trier, No. 2	7 50
20 Wellesley, No. 1	12 50
40 Wellesley, No. 2	8 00
200 Veilchenblau, No. 1	6 00
400 Veilchenblau, No. 2	4 00
700 White Cochet, No. 1	12 50
500 White Cochet, No. 2	8 00
200 Wm. R. Smith, No. 1	15 00
150 Wm. R. Smith, No. 2	10 00
500 White Dorothy Perkins, No. 1	7 50
400 White Dorothy Perkins, No. 2	5 00
800 White Rambler, No. 1	7 50
400 White Rambler, No. 2	5 00

ROSES, Budded

	Per 100
300 American Beauty, No. 1	$15 0
200 Frau Karl Druschki, No. 1	10 00
200 La France, No. 1	12 50
300 Mad. Caroline Testout, No. 1	15 00
200 Marechal Neil, No. 1	15 00
100 Marechal Neil, No. 2	$ 10 00

These, with the exception of Marechal Neil, all Holland grown.

TREE ROSES

Holland grown, just arrived, in prime condition, per 100 ....$35 00

160 Baby Rambler	30 Glorie Dijon	25 Mrs. John Laing
130 Frau Karl Druschki	35 Gruss aus Teplitz	25 Mad. Caroline Testout
185 Mrs. Cutbush	135 Magna Charta	25 Perle des Blanches

"LINING OUT" STOCK

Ornamental Trees, Shrubs, Deciduous and Evergreen, Climbers

For Transplanting to Nursery Row

We are offering a longer list of this class of stock than usual. All Imported stocks were personally inspected in France and Holland by a member of our firm. Everything will be strictly up to the grade specified.

We urge EARLY ORDERS on this class of stock. Can carry in storage until you want delivery, but will not offer this stock in boxed lots from our distributing points, and this list will not appear in our later Bulletins. WE MAKE NO CHARGE FOR PACKING THIS TRANSPLANTING STOCK, prices include proper packing in paper lined cases.

	Per 100	Per 1000
ALTHEA, Mixed Seedlings, 1 year, 3-16 caliper, cut back to 6 inches of wood, especially grown for grafting		$ 3 50
ALTHEA, Named Sorts, 1 to 2 feet		25 00

Admiral Dewey, pure double white	Duchess de Brabant, double dark red
Amplissima, double vinous rose	Jeanne de Arc, double pure white
Amemonaeflorus, double red	Monstrosus, semi-double white
Ardens, double violet	Rubis, single red
Boule de Feu, double red	Souv. Chas. Breton, single violet
Carnea Plena, semi-double flesh	

	Per 100	Per 1000
ALTHEA, Totus Albus, single pure white		30 00
AMPELOPSIS, Veitchii, 2 year, transplanted		25 00
ACER, Dasycarpum, Silver Maple, 1 year, 18 to 24 inches		6 00
12 to 18 inches		4 50
ACER, Dasycarpum Wieri, Wier's Cut Leaf Maple, 2 year. 3 to 4 feet	$6 00	
ACER, Palmatum, Japan Maple, 2 year, 12 to 15 inches	5 00	
ACER, Platanoides, Norway Maple, 2 year, 2½ to 3 feet	3 50	
ACER, Saccharum, Sugar Maple, 1 year, 6 to 12 inches	3 50	
BERBERIS, Purpurea, Purple Leaf Barberry, 3 year, 12 to 15 inches		25 00
8 to 12 inches		20 00
BERBERIS, Thunbergii, Japan Barberry, 1 year, 8 to 12 inches		10 00
6 to 10 inches		8 50
BERBERIS, Vulgaris, Green Barberry, 2 year, 12 to 15 inches		20 00
BERBERIS, Buxifolia, Box Leaved Barberry, 2 year, 12 to 18 inches	3 00	
BUXUS, Sempervirens, Tree Box, 3 year, 8 to 12 inches		35 00
BETULA, Alba, White Birch, 2 year, 2 feet		15 00
CALYCANTHUS, Floridus, 1 year, 8 to 15 inches		15 00
CORNUS, Alba, Red Branched Dogwood, 1 year, 8 to 15 inches	2 50	
CORNUS, Florida, White Flowering Dogwood, 1 year, 6 to 12 inches, transplanted		35 00
CERCIS, Canadensis, Judas Tree, 2 year, 18 to 24 inches		30 00
CLEMATIS, Paniculata, 1 year, potted	3 75	
CYDONIA, Japonica, Japan Quince, 3 year, 12 to 18 inches	3 00	
2 year, 8 to 12 inches		17 50
DEUTZIA, Pride of Rochester, 1 year, 8 to 15 inches		20 00
EUONYMUS, Alatus, 2 year, transplanted, 8 to 12 inches	4 50	
1 year, 4 to 6 inches		25 00
EUONYMUS, Japonica, 1 year, 6 to 12 inches		35 00
EUONYMUS, Radicans, 1 year, 6 to 12 inches		15 00
EXOCHORDA, Grandiflora, 2 year, 8 to 15 inches		30 00
FRAXINUS, Americana. Am. White Ash, 2 year, 2 to 3 feet		25 00
FORSYTHIA, Intermedia, 1 year, 12 to 18 inches		20 00
FORSYTHIA, Suspensa, 1 year, 12 to 18 inches	2 50	
FORSYTHIA, Viridissima, 1 year, 12 to 18 inches		20 00
GARDENIA, Cape Jasmine, 2 year, 12 to 15 inches	7 00	
1 year, 4 to 6 inches	3 50	
GINKGO, Biloba, Maidenhair Tree, 2 year, 12 to 15 inches		30 00
HYDRANGEA, A. Sterilis, Hills of Snow, 1 year, 8 to 15 inches	4 50	
HYDRANGEA, P. G., 2 year, 12 to 15 inches, transplanted		37 50
1 year, 8 to 12 inches, transplanted		27 50
HYPERICUM, Calycinum, 2 year, 6 to 12 inches		25 00
HYPERICUM, Moserianum, 2 year, 6 to 12 inches		30 00
LAGERSTROEMIA, Indica, Crepe Myrtle, 1 year, 8 to 15 inches	4 00	
1 year, 4 to 6 inches		20 00
LIGUSTRUM, Amurense "South," Southern Evergreen Privet, 1 year, 8 to 15 inches		17 50

11

	Per 100	Per 1000
LIGUSTRUM, Amurense "North," Hardy Amoor River Privet, 1 year, 8 to 15 inches		20 00
LIGTSTRUM, Ibota, 1 year, 8 to 15 inches		17 50
LIGUSTRUM, Japonica, Japan Privet, 2 year, 8 to 12 inches		25 00
LIGUSTRUM, Ovalifolium, California Privet, 1 year, 8 to 12 inches		7 50
LONICERA, Halleana, Hall's Honeysuckle, 2 year, cut back to 12 inches		15 00
LONICERA, Punicea, Scarlet Trumpet Honeysuckle, 1 year, cut back to 12 inches		20 00
LONICERA, Sinensis, Chinese Honeysuckle, 2 year, cut back to 12 inches		20 00
LONICERA, Tartarica Alba, White Tartarian Honeysuckle, 2 year, 8 to 15 inches		30 00
LONICERA, Tartarica Rosea, Red Tartarian Honeysuckle, 2 year, 8 to 15 inches		25 00
MAGNOLIA, Acuminata, 1 year, 1 to 2 feet	2 00	
MAGNOLIA, Grandiflora, 6 to 12 inches	4 00	
MAGNOLIA, Tripetala, 1 year, 1 to 2 feet	2 00	
MELIA, Azederach Umbraculiformis, Chinese Umbrella, 1 year, 1 to 2 feet		15 00
PHILADELPHUS, named varieties, Syringa or Mock Orange, 2 year, 8 to 15 inches		25 00

    Coronarius   Dianthiflorus Plenus   Grandiflorus
    Lemoinei   Mont Blanc

	Per 100	Per 1000
PLATANUS, Occidentalis, American Sycamore, 1 year, 18 to 24 inches		8 00
PLATANUS, Orientalis, European Sycamore, Oriental Plane, 2 year, 2 to 3 feet		37 50
POPULUS, Fastigiata, Lombardy Poplar, 4 to 5 feet		40 00
3 to 4 feet		35 00
2 to 3 feet		15 00
POPULUS, Molinifera, Carolina Poplar, 4 to 5 feet		20 00
3 to 4 feet		15 00
2 to 3 feet		10 00
RHUS, Cotinus, Purple Fringe, 2 year, 8 to 15 inches		20 00
SPIREA, Anthony Waterer, 3 year, 6 to 12 inches		30 00
2 year, 6 to 12 inches		22 50
SPIREA, Prunifolia, 2 year, 8 to 15 inches		30 00
SPIREA, Thunbergii, 2 year, 8 to 15 inches		20 00
SPIREA VAN HOUTTE, 1 year, 1 to 2 feet		17 50
SYMPHORICARPOS, Vulgaris, Coral Berry, 1 year, 8 to 12 inches		15 00
SYRINGA, Vulgaris, Purple Lilac, 2 year, 12 to 15 inches		20 00
SYRINGA, Vulgaris Alba, White Lilac, 2 year, 8 to 12 inches		25 00
VIBURNUM, Opulus Sterilis, 2 year, 8 to 12 inches		30 00
WEIGELIA, Candida. 2 year, 8 to 15 inches		30 00
WEIGELIA, Eva Rathke, 2 year, 8 to 15 inches		50 00
WEIGELIA, Rosea, 2 year, 8 to 15 inches		35 00
WEIGELIA, Variegata, 2 year, 6 to 12 inches		30 00
WISTARIA, Sinensis, Chinese Purple Wistaria, 2 year, Layers	5 00	
WISTARIA, Sinensis Alba, Chinese White Wistaria, 2 year, Layers	6 00	

FRUIT TREE SEEDLINGS

The American grown seedlings are now in stock in fine order and can ship on short notice. The Imported seedlings are arriving from Europe and by the time this list reaches you, almost all items will be in stock. All seedlings under this heading are DELIVERED F. O. B. CARS HERE, WELL PACKED IN PAPER LINED BOXES at prices named.

	Per 1000
Apple, American Grown, No. 1, 3-16 and up, straight roots	$ 7 50
Apple, American Grown, No. 2, 2-16 to 3,16, straight roots	3 50
Apple, French Grown, Imported, No. 1, 5 to 7 mm, branched roots	7 50

    (The No. 1 and No. 2 straight roots are best for piece root grafting, the French branched roots are best for whole root grafts and for budding. The French measure, mm, means millimeters, of which there are 25 to one inch.)

	Per 1000
Pear, Japan, American Grown, No. 2, 2-16 to 3-16, too small for grafting	7 50
Pear, French, American Grown, No. 1, 3-16 and up, mostly straight roots	9 00
Pear, French, Imported, No. 1, 5 to 7 mm, branched roots	8 00
Pear, French, Imported, No. 2, 3 to 5 mm	4 50

    (The No. 2 French, Imported, are too light for grafting)

	Per 1000
Cherry, Mahaleb, Imported, No. 1, 5 to 10 mm	10 00
Cherry, Mahaleb, Imported, No. 2, 3 to 5 mm	6 25
Plum, Myrobolan, No. 1, Imported, 5 to 10 mm	12 50
Plum, Myrobolan, No. 2, Imported, 3 to 5 mm	9 00
Quince, Angers, Imported, 5 to 7 mm	7 00
Mulberry, Russian, 1 year seedlings, 12 to 18 inches, about 3-16 inches	6 00
Chestnut, Spanish, Imported, 1 year, 6 to 12 inches, seedlings	15 00
Chestnut, Spanish, Imported, 2 year, 12 to 18 inches, seedlings	20 00
Walnut, English, Imported, 1 year, 4 to 6 inches, seedlings	25 00
Walnut, English, 2 year, 6 to 12 inches, seedlings	30 00
Walnut, Japan, American grown, 2 year, 6 to 12 inches, seedlings	20 00

EVERGREEN SHRUBS

	Per 10	Per 100
25 Abelia, Grandiflora, 15 to 18 inches	$ 2 50	
100 Buxus; Arborescens, 2 to 3 feet, trimmed pyramids	10 00	
600 Buxus, Suffruticosa, (Dwarf Box) 4 to 6 inches		$ 5 00
50 Cotoneaster, Augustifolia, 2 to 3 feet	1 50	
300 Euonymus, Japonica; 12 to 18 inches		12 50
200 Gardenia, (Cape Jasmine) 18 to 24 inches		17 50
300 Gardenia, (Cape Jasmine) 12 to 18 inches		12 50
50 Laurocerasus (English Laurel) 18 to 24 inches	2 50	
200 Laurocerasus, (English Laurel) 12 to 18 inches		20 00
200 Ligustrum. Japonicum, 12 to 18 inches		10 00
50 Ligustrum, Jap. Macrophyllum, 18 to 24 inches	3 00	
100 Ligustrum, Jap. Macrophyllum, 12 to 18 inches	2 00	
100 Rhododendron, Ponticium, 18 inches, well budded	6 50	

NOTE—If wanted Balled add 5 cents per plant.

NURSERYMEN'S SUPPLIES

PROMPT SHIPMENT

All supply orders (except printed matter) are usually shipped next train after receipt. We try to carry a complete stock at all times. Our location at Chase gives us unsurpassed facilities for quick action on rush orders—two lines of railway, ten trains per day stopping here.

KNIVES

Made especially for us by a manufacturer who is "fussy" about the quality of his output. Have used and handled these knives for twenty years.

PRUNING—Chase's Flat Handle Pruner—The strongest pruning knife made, handle composed of two halves hardwood riveted through the blade which extends full length, see cut above. Full length 7¼ inches. If you can break the handle on this knife we will replace it without cost. The metal is high-class. Price, 35c each, $3.50 per dozen postpaid; $3.20 per dozen by freight or express.

PRUNING—C. A. G. Pruner—Stationary handle; full length 8 ins., length of blade 3⅜ ins. Handle, hardwood; blade entered deep and fastened by tang through full length of handle, making a strong knife. 30c each, $3.20 per doz. postpaid; $2.85 per dozen by freight or express.

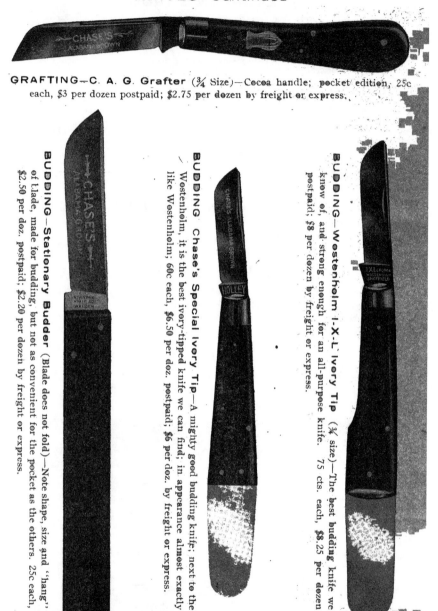

GRAFTING—C. A. G. Grafter (¾ Size)—Cocoa handle; pocket edition, 25c each, $3 per dozen postpaid; $2.75 per dozen by freight or express.

BUDDING—Westenholm I·X·L' Ivory Tip (¾ size)—The best budding knife we know of, and strong enough for an all-purpose knife. 75 cts. each, $8.25 per dozen postpaid; $8 per dozen by freight or express.

BUDDING Chase's Special Ivory Tip—A mighty good budding knife; next to the Westenholm, it is the best ivory-tipped knife we can find; in appearance almost exactly like Westenholm; 60c each, $6.50 per doz. postpaid; $6 per doz. by freight or express.

BUDDING—Stationary Budder (Blade does not fold)—Note shape, size and "hang" of blade, made for budding, but not as convenient for the pocket as the others. 25c each, $2.50 per doz. postpaid; $2.20 per dozen by freight or express.

Special Notice—All postpaid prices on supplies are based on the old merchandise rate, we will apply Parcel Post rates and where there is a saving effected, you will get the benefit. The difference between the old merchandise rate and the new rate will be credited on invoice, or returned to you if you have remitted cash with order.

PRUNING SHEARS

The Watch Spring French Shears stand at the head of the list for making cuttings of all kinds. For this work the 8 inch size is just right. For cutting back seedlings to the bud or any heavy work the 9 inch is recommended.

Watch Spring, French, 8 inch—Per pair postpaid, $1.35; per dozen pairs freight or express (weight per dozen pairs 7 lbs.) $14.50.

Watch Spring, French, 9 inch—Per pair postpaid, $1.70; per dozen pairs freight or express (weight per dozen pairs 11 lbs.) $17.00.

English Pattern, 8 inch One of the best made shears in the market; an extra blade with each. Heavy long brass spring that will last as long as the shears. $1.90 per pair postpaid.

Ladies' German, 6 inch, full nickel plated. Volute spring. Not large enough for general use. High grade, beautifully finished, large enough for use about rose bushes or shrubs in the garden, or for light work. 75c per pair, postpaid; $8.00 per dozen pairs by express or freight. Weight per dozen pairs, 2¾ lbs.

American Make, 9 inch—Good cheap shears, strong, well made, weight 17 ounces. Volute steel spring. 65c per pair, postpaid. Per dozen pairs, $5.75, by freight or express, per half dozen $3.00, per pair, 50c. The best low priced all rround pruning shear we know of.

15

Box Lining Paper—Now universally · used by progressive · nurserymen; risky business to pack in unlined boxes. This paper is tough, resists a good deal of moisture, almost waterproof. Helps keep out heat as well as frost, protects contents of box from drying winds. Put up in rolls, 30, 36 and 40 inches wide, about 100 pounds in a roll. One roll of 40 inch will completely line about 27 full size cases. This is not the lowest priced paper on the market, but our experience proves it the most economical. We cannot break rolls. Per pound, 4½ cents.

Ames Nursery Spade—D handle, double strapped full length of handle, tapered nursery spade; size of blade 12¾ x 7½ x 5½ ; weight, 9 pounds. $1.50 each, $18.00 per dozen. SPADE HANDLES for above spade. These handles are bent to fit' and riveted. 40 cents each, $4.50 per dozen.

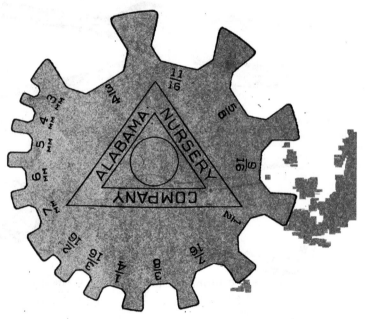

Improved Tree Guage—Price, any quantity, 50 cents each. Made from "Sheradised" steel (a new process of treating steel); absolutely rust-proof; both sides marked alike; always right side up; guaranteed accurate to within one-hundredth of an inch; indestructible; easy to read.

Chemicals for Fumigating—CYANIDE OF POTASH (Merck & Co.'s 98 per cent). In original sealed tin packages. 1 lb. cans, 45 cts; 5 lb. cans, $1.85. Cyanide of Potash is excluded from the mails; but can be shipped by express or frt.
SULPHURIC ACID. (Specific gravity, 1.83). Large, glass-stopped bottles, securely packed in cases ready for shipment. 10 lb. bottle, $1.20; 15 lb. bottle $1.50. Sulphuric acid cannot be shipped by express, but can be shipped by freight.

Raffia—We use the best Raffia we can buy, regardless of its cost. because, for nurserymen's use, the best is most economical. Per lb. by mail, postpaid, 30 cents, 10 to 50 lbs. per lb. f. o. b. Chase, 13½ cents. 100 lbs, per lb. f. o. b. Chase, 12½ cents. Ask for prices on bale lots (about 220 lbs.)

Cordage, Twines, Etc —FLAX SAIL TWINE.   For sewing burlap; put up in skeins, per pound, 30 cents.

TWO-PLY SISAL CORD (breaking strength 170 pounds) For heavy express bales; on reels of about 50 pounds each, per pound 10½ cts.   We cannot sell less than a reel.

FOUR-PLY WOOL-TWINE—For tying trees in bundles; put up in balls weighing about one pound each; packed about 120 pounds in a bale.   In bale lots, per pound, 10½ cts., in less than bale lots, per pound, 11½ cents.

TARRED SISAL YARN or LATH CORD.   In coils. Good for tying trees for storage or cellars.   About 100 pounds to a coil.   Per lb. 11½c, (Will sell any amount wanted.)

Grafting Thread Put up in balls and packed 20 balls to the box.   A box of twenty balls will wrap about 40,000 average grafts.

Price per Ball unwaxed	8c
Price per Ball waxed	12c
Price per box 20 Balls unwaxed	$1.25
Price per box 20 balls waxed	1.90

(If mailed, add 2c ball unwaxed and 5c ball waxed)

The above illustration shows a ball of our grafting thread with a pencil run through the hole in the center.   Many nurserymen prefer to suspend the ball of grafting thread from a wire to be unwound as it is used.   We prefer to keep the grafting thread in warm water while it is being used, as described below. This can be used either way.

· To Keep Grafting Thread in Good Condition While Using

Put a ball of waxed grafting thread into a quart cup or pan (a tomato can will do) fill it half full of water and arrange over a lighted lamp or small oil stove to keep the water warm.

"Scrap Burlap"—Second hand pieces 24 inches square and upward, bales of 100 pounds, per pound, 4½ cents.

Needles for Sewing Burlap—Five-inch, extra quality, large eye, 40c per dozen; 5 inch common, 25 cents per dozen.

Labels—PLAIN IRON WIRED.   3½ in. plain, 1000 to package, 75 cents per 1000, by freight or express; in 5000 lots, 70 cents per 1000; in 10,000 lots, 65 cents per 1000.   COPPER WIRED, size same as above, add 15 cents per 1000.

Chase's "Dig Ezy" Hoe—This is a thoroughbred.   It's long and narrow "snout" makes it one of the best Nursery Weeding Hoes we have ever used, and it is also strong enough to grub out seedlings.   This hoe is not too heavy.   Balanced just right.   Double riveted, 65c each, $5.50 per dozen.   Will sell half doz. at doz. rate.

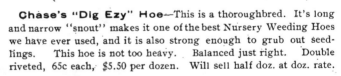

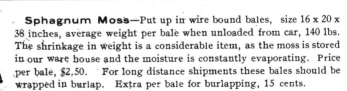

Sphagnum Moss—Put up in wire bound bales, size 16 x 20 x 38 inches, average weight per bale when unloaded from car, 140 lbs. The shrinkage in weight is a considerable item, as the moss is stored in our ware house and the moisture is constantly evaporating.   Price per bale, $2.50.   For long distance shipments these bales should be wrapped in burlap.   Extra per bale for burlapping, 15 cents.

Steel Box Straps—One inch wide, 9 inches long, thin, soft steel, strong enough to hold the heaviest box. You can drive an ordinary nail through it without punching. About 2800 pieces in 100 pounds. Less than 50 pounds, per lb. 5c; 50 pound boxes, per box, $2.25; 100 pound boxes, per box, $4.00.

Alabama Mule Skin Mittens A leather mitten with separate sheath for forefinger, the other three fingers in one sheath. Made from mule skin, nearly as durable as buckskin, at one-fourth the cost. Single pair, by mail, 40 cts. postpaid; one dozen pairs, by freight or express, $3.50.

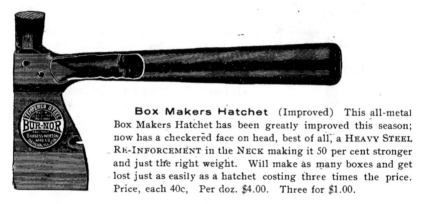

Box Makers Hatchet (Improved) This all-metal Box Makers Hatchet has been greatly improved this season; now has a checkered face on head, best of all, a HEAVY STEEL RE-INFORCEMENT in the NECK making it 50 per cent stronger and just the right weight. Will make as many boxes and get lost just as easily as a hatchet costing three times the price. Price, each 40c, Per doz. $4.00. Three for $1.00.

Automatic Tacking Machine

For fastening tags or cards to tree boxes, cars, etc. The slickest little labor saver in our packing house. No hunting for tacks, no finger pricks, fumbling for hammer or lost motion. Just lay it on top of tag or card and tap the knob with palm of hand, a light tap, quick as lightning, will tag a box so quickly and easily that it is a joy to do it. Instead of round headed tacks 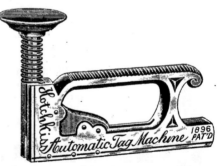 this little machine automatically staples the tag or card in place. Guaranteed to work on any wood. Money back if not satisfactory; will ship on thirty days trial to any responsible nurseryman. Machine guaranteed against breakage for three years. Machine, each $1.50: Postpaid, $1.80; Staples per box of 5000, $1.50: Postpaid $1.70

NOTICE—We will give you the benefit of the DOZEN RATE on all orders for Knives, Shears, Mule Skin Mittens, etc., when ordered in half-dozen lots.

OFFICE SUPPLIES

Order Books—Your name and address printed, 100 orders to book, best quality, heavy glazed paper, latest form. Sample sheet free for the asking. Not less than 500. $2.50 for 500 (5 books), Postage extra; $3.25 per 1000 (10 books) postage extra. Postage extra 5c per book. Always give plain copy of firm name and address so that no mistake in printing will occur.

Delivery Books - Bound in paper cover, ruled, showing name of customer, post office address, amount of order, how settled, etc. For 24 accounts, 50 cents per dozen postpaid; for 72 accounts, 75 cents per dozen postpaid; for 120 accounts, 85 cents per dozen postpaid; for 168 accounts, $1.00 per dozen postpaid. Half dozen at dozen rates, Inexpensive and mighty handy.

Shipping Tags—Printed to order, strung ready for use. Three sizes, two qualities, all have reinforced eyelets.

Standard Quality, Reinforced Eyelets
A better tag than is usually used

		Per 500	Per 1000
Size No. 5.	2½x4¾ inches, printed on one side	$2 10	$3 20
	Printed on two sides	3 10	4 45
Size No. 7.	2⅞x5¾ inches, printed on one side	2 15	3 30
	Printed on two sides	3 15	4 55
Size No. 8.	3⅛x6⅜ inches, printed on one side	2 25	3 35
	Printed on two sides	3 25	4 65

Note the new size (No. 8) this season. This tag has plenty of room for address and Inspection Certificate on one side without crowding.

Extra Quality, Waterproof, Brass Bound Eyelets
THE BEST TAG WE KNOW OF

		Per 500	Per 1000
Size No. 5.	2½x4¾ inches, printed on one side	$2 35	$3 65
	Printed on two sides	3 35	4 90
Size No. 7.	2⅞x5¾ inches, printed on one side	2 40	3 80
	Printed on two sides	3 40	5 05

Always send copy showing how tags are to be printed. Samples on request.

GREAT GRIP NUT SHELLER
A Real Nut Cracker at Last

Not strictly speaking a nursery tool, but all nurserymen like nuts, and you have like ourselves used the old style nut crackers, pinched your fingers. smashed the meat of the nut all to pieces, lost your temper and damaged your religion. In offering this little implement we are really doing missionary work. It is a dandy. Beautifully made, will last a life-time; constructed on new and scientific lines. So arranged that the jaws with their great grip, never close fully; will receive a table nut of any size and variety, and crack the shell only, bringing out the meat whole. Will handle castana ("nigger toes") with the same ease that it shells a pecan. Heavily nickeled, an ornament to any table. Price each, postpaid, $1.60; by freight or express with other goods. $1.50. Money back without a word to any dissatisfied user.